# INSPIRATIONAL STEW:

150 Poems, Quotations and Maxims For Teachers, Parents and Caregivers to Encourage and Inspire Young People

*Claritha D. Ingram*

Copyright © 2014 by Claritha D. Ingram
All rights reserved.

Published in the United States by SSCOMM Publishing,
A division of SSCOMM, Inc.
Memphis, Tennessee 38175-3897
www.sscommpr.com | info@sscommpr.com

Library of Congress Control Number: 2014947800

ISBN-13: 978-0-9906512-0-8
ISBN-10: 0990651207

Cover design by Frederick Virgous
Book layout and editing by Florence M. Howard

# DEDICATION

This book is dedicated to children all over the world to inspire and encourage them to embrace education and become lifelong learners who are capable of achieving their dream to enhance the future of the world in which they live and, in addition to that, to show each one the beauty and intelligence they have within.

# PREFACE

Claritha Draper Ingram is a retired classroom teacher with 35 years of teaching experience. The majority of the children she taught were from underserved and at risk neighborhoods. For 30 years, she taught kindergarten through sixth grade and enjoyed every day until retirement. Upon her retirement, she continued to teach by accepting long-term substitute positions in middle schools for five years. She enjoyed teaching, mentoring and inspiring students using a positive approach -- words and verses to make them think and to motivate them to use their time wisely and take charge of their destiny. When she couldn't find the kinds of poems she wanted, she wrote them.

This positive approach was a ritual she used everyday before instruction began and she continued to incorporate encouraging messages throughout the day, when needed, to modify inappropriate behavior or encourage academic performance. As young minds opened daily to new learning, she encouraged students with the belief that they could climb the highest mountain and fly pass the moon and stars in a world of possibility with a good education. She was able to do this by using an encouraging voice to share positive poems and enriching expressions each day.

Her goal was to give young scholars a stimulus through positive messages and poems that would help them to understand what they were capable of achieving in life *with a good education* and without which they would not be able to maximize their potential to the fullest. The effectiveness of her approach was reflected in her ability to empower students with self-assurance, while molding and beautifying character at the same time. For example, the enthusiasm of the students for learning was such that they began sharing and working cooperatively together without conflict.

Her most gratifying reward was the encouraging feedback from parents, co-workers and administrators plus positive changes in the students themselves.

# ACKNOWLEDGMENTS

I would like to thank all my students who were inspired by the daily ritual of reciting positive poems, motivational messages and educational catch-phrases. I would like to thank parents for their positive feedback, and my mom who listened patiently as I read each poem to her before sharing with my students. I would like to thank my sisters for their encouraging support. Finally, I thank my editor Florence M. Howard for her dedication to purpose and to all my friends and coworkers who supported and encouraged me along the way.

# CONTENTS

Preface
Acknowledgments
Introduction

**Guiding Students with Encouraging Words .........19**

The Art of Imagination by Wilferd A. Peterson
The Art of Listening by Wilferd A. Peterson
~
Inspiration
Inspirational Stew
Witty Wisdom
Think About It
Spoken Words
From A Teacher To Students
Are You Thinking
A Voice That Sings
Food For Thought
Invisible Shadows
Creative Thinking
~
Teaching Tips

**Poems for the Hearts and Minds
of Young Scholars……………………….…………39**

It's Up To You
Everyone Can't Be In The Front Row

Scoring
Confident
The Buzz
Education Is
Delight Yourself
What Is Knowledge?
Press Forward
It's Your Fault
Dreams
Change
Think
Rules and Procedures
Gateway To Success
A Pathway To Nowhere
A Powerful Tool
Priceless Gem
You Are History In The Making
Reflections
I Am In Charge
Aim High
Attitude
Manage Your Education
Find Your Light
Door of Opportunity
Self-Promotion
You Want Power?
Direct Your Future
Confession
If by Rudyard Kipling
Hold Fast to Dreams by Langston Hughes
My People by Langston Hughes

Book Power
Promote Yourself, Be Your Own Portfolio
and Resume, Blow Your Own Horn
The Best You Can Be
Special
The Classroom
Possibility
Why Am I Here?
What's Blocking the Learning
Guidance
What If
All About Me
My Profile
I Am The Greatest
Make It Happen
The Builder
LifeLong Learner
Passionate
Inner Thoughts
I Am Ready
Word Power
Moving Forward
Significant
I Got This

**A Positive Approach to Classroom Management...101**
Literary Gems, Thoughts to Ponder,
Words to Live By

**Educational Catch-Phrases............................123**
Education Makes It Happen

# INTRODUCTION

Teaching students can be challenging, and classroom management can be an even bigger challenge. A teacher can work extremely hard preparing class rules and reminding students of expectations and procedures. Unfortunately, inappropriate conduct often takes center stage. Rules and consequences are okay to control this behavior for a short period of time. However, students soon become immune to them over a period of time. When the fear of misbehaving is no longer a concern, inappropriate behavior resurfaces. Teaching and learning are then sacrificed for discipline.

Nevertheless, using a positive approach, you will capture their attention. The goal is to keep students engaged in learning and manage classroom discipline at the same time. Now the big question is: How do you do it?

## A Positive Approach

By incorporating motivational poems and messages into instruction every morning before you begin, you can align students' thoughts with words of encouragement to uplift their spirits. Articulating the right words that reach out to young minds can have a powerful and positive influence on how a child behaves and performs in the classroom. This is something children can feel within. It is meaningful and forms a foundation for their strength to push harder to achieve their best level of proficiency. Some students will be reluctant at first but add a daily deposit of motivational wisdom; and, "BINGO," they will begin to accept the wisdom as truth. Moreover, they will start thinking on a different level about their education, character and self-worth. This positive activity needs to take place in homes, classrooms, and communities: **"It takes a village to raise a child."** *(African proverb)*

With the right tone of voice and combination of the right words – teachers, parents, and all others who work and care for children can make them feel good about themselves when you share their beauty and smarts within. Few things bring more anticipation, joy and excitement than when children discover they are dripping with hidden possibilities along with the fact that they are fantastically amazing, remarkable and unique. **"The strength of an education lies not in the number of children but in the hearts and souls you inspire to succeed every day."**

## Key Steps

Consistency is the hero in everyone's life. In order to build a visual memory of the poems, select one weekly and let the children recite it daily as you navigate them through each verse. After that, encourage them to chime in and be creative using expressive voices and gestures. This provides an opportunity to make them feel good about who they are regardless of the obstacles they face in the classroom or in the community. Next, display the poem somewhere so that it is a readily available message. This opens the territory to continually remind students about the message throughout the day and to maintain discipline. For example, to avoid interrupting instruction, I used the expressions on note cards. When students were playing around or ignoring the lesson, I would walk and place on their desk a note that spoke to the inappropriate behavior. I did not stop instruction to discuss the issue. After the note card was read, attention was quickly recaptured as the student moved forward with the learning. After class or when students were working independently, those students with cards were called to "the situation table" to discuss the problem. If the problem continued, a parent conference was called. Three or more note cards during a six-week grading period determined the conduct grade.

Also, parents and community helpers working with children can use expressions to encourage a commitment to education.

## A Word to Educators

Try setting a positive tone for learning in your classroom by starting a child's day with words of encouragement. This stimulates the imagination and improves their ability to focus on the learning. It helps them relax, too, and takes their minds off outside problems (that are going on inside their heads). As a result, they soon forget about outside matters.

Every child must be wakened to the fact that they have a mixture of unbelievable instincts and potential -- if they put forth the effort, believe in their ability, and focus on learning. I believe it would be safe to say they will become more fully aware and conscious of this potential as they continue to travel through school grades.

Educators, their minds are ready. The classroom is where children's dreams and teachers' expertise collide. So, strive to excite their hearts and reveal their genius.

## A Word to Parents

Now, parents, imagine if you were to use your voice and pen to continue to reinforce positive communication. Consider nudging the conscious mind of your child to behave their best and do their best every day. This will boost your child's spirit. Dare to unlock their potential!

One simple way that you can do this is to select a poem or an expression every day. Read it with them then have them clip it and attach it to the refrigerator, wall, mirror or anywhere in the home where it is readily visible for reading. Discuss it, making sure they focus on the words and their meaning. Have them read it over again and again until they claim the text as truth. This will redouble your effort to keep nudging their subconscious to remind them of their genius. Some children can be tough for sure but they also can be truly transformed. A little encouragement goes a long, long way.

Another eye-opening way parents can employ poems and expressions is by using "confidence notes." Select a text, short poem or stanza that praises, encourages self-confidence, or addresses academics. Add a personal touch and place the note of confidence in their pocket, backpack, purse, lunch bag, pencil box or notebook. This surprise will put a big, big smile on their face when it is pulled out and read. Confidence notes can be a great tool and your secret weapon in focusing on what really matters: Education is a priority.

## A Word to Caregivers

Finally, custodial caregivers of children in the community, nurture young minds by using the expressions and poems from the book in whatever way you want and desire. Collaborate with your charges to encourage, motivate and inspire them. This cooperative effort can be an exciting one for each child.

## About This Book

Positive words do not come naturally for some when communicating with students, correcting behavior or changing academic performance. Sometimes it is hard to find the right words to say. With that in mind, I decided to share a collection of poems and expressions I used to speak to students giving them that little nudge needed to light the fire of "HOPE." Most of the poems were written by the author, an educator with years and years of experience who has also worked as a school librarian.

Until you find your own way of lifting children's spirits, this resource can serve as a guide and a focus for inspiration. In it, you will find an arousing collection of sweet and tasty inspirational poems dripping with encouragement, enveloped with hope. The poetry is separated into two segments: "Guiding Students with Encouraging Words" and "Poems for the Hearts and Minds of Young Scholars."

Next, dive right into the time-honored, time-tested wisdom of "A Positive Approach to Classroom Management." This segment offers specially selected literary gems, thoughts to ponder and words to live by. Each quotation speaks to character, perseverance, and reassurance. Take a peek inside the pages, this book is a page turner. You can hardly wait to read the next poem or expression. Read and enjoy. While reading you will find yourself saying, "Wow, this is great!" Or, "This is exactly what I need; I know what I can do with this one!" And maybe even, "A-ha, I think I can use most of these to encourage students."

*Inspirational Stew* is a pick-and-choose resource for teachers, parents and caregivers. You can read straight through or select sections to assist in correcting behavior or improving academic performance. Its positive messages will help you tremendously. My intent is to reach out to the majority of ingenious thinkers and doers with endlessly curious minds sitting in classrooms every day. I wrote this book to let them know that, with a good education, they are capable of achieving their dreams and enhancing their futures. I wrote many of the poems and positive expressions in the book myself. A few poems were inspired by various articles and magazine ads collected throughout my teaching career. Many of the original authors of the literary gems, quotations and maxims are unknown; however, authors are listed wherever possible. I want to acknowledge with appreciation those authors for their words of inspirational wisdom.

# GUIDING STUDENTS

# WITH

# ENCOURAGING WORDS

# THE ART OF IMAGINATION

"**IMAGINATION,**" said Einstein, "is more powerful than knowledge."

**IMAGINATION** enlarges your vision, stretches the mind, challenges the impossible. Without IMAGINATION, thought comes to a halt!

**YOU AWAKEN** your imagination through the driving power of curiosity and discontent.

**YOU LIGHT UP** your imagination by stroking your mental fires through the senses -- eyes, nose, muscles, skin. You spur your imagination by giving it abundant data with which to work.

**YOUR IMAGINATION** becomes for you a magic lamp with which to explore the darkness of the unknown, that you may chart new paths to old goals.

**YOU RECOGNIZE** the reality of facts, but you use your imagination to penetrate beneath them and to project your thoughts beyond them in your search for creative answers to problems.

**IMAGINATION,** through your imagination you touch and express the inspiration of the infinite.

**IMAGINATION,** in the words of Shakespeare, "gives to airy nothing a local habitation and a name." You reach into sky to grasp an idea, then you bring it down to earth and make it work.

**YOU LEARN** from the great master of imagination, Thomas Edison, who when asked the secret of inventive genius replied, "I'll listen from within."

**YOU USE YOUR IMAGINATION** to look at everything with fresh eyes, as though you had just come forth from a dark tunnel into the light of day.

*~ Wilferd A. Peterson*

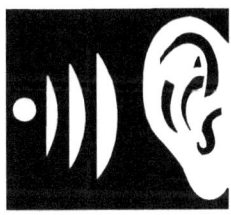

# THE ART OF LISTENING

The key to the art of listening is selectivity.... You stand guard at the ear-gateway to your mind, heart and spirit. You decide what you will accept ...

- Listen to the good. Tune your ears to love, hope, and courage. Tune out gossip, fear and resentment.

- Listen with your eyes. Let your imagination make real the "sound" expressed in a novel, a picture, a poem.

- Listen with patience. Do not hurry the other person. Show him the courtesy of listening to what he has to say, no matter how much you may disagree, you may learn something.

- Listen with your heart. Put yourself in the other person's place and try to hear the problem in your heart.

- Listen for growth. Be an inquisitive listener. Ask questions. Everyone has something to say which will help you to grow.

- Listen to yourself. Listen to your deepest yearnings, your highest aspiration, your noblest impulses. Listen to the better person within you.

- Listen with depth. Be still and meditate. Listen with the ear of intuition for the inspiration of the infinite.

*~ Wilferd A. Peterson*

# INSPIRATION

Inspiration, unbelievable,
Too often forgotten,
Planted in rows like cabbage,
Sit promises of tomorrow,
In spite of adversities,
Inside each head are,
Hidden strengths, unknown expectations.

Inspiration reenergizes
As knowledge pours in taking root
It's exhilarating to see,
Intelligent minds come together
Waiting to be cultivated.

Inspiration excites,
It's just wonderful,
It's unbelievable.
Amazingly enthusiastic scholars
Take on challenges and find
Value in knowledge,
A passion for learning.

INSPIRATION IS UNBELIEVABLE!
*"WISDOM THAT ENCOURAGES
IS CLOTHING FOR THE UNBELIEVABLE."*

*Claritha D. Ingram*

## INSPIRATIONAL STEW

There is lots of inspiration in my stew,
No meat, potatoes, tomatoes,
Celery or carrots to chew
Just turn the pages
In this book and peek inside,
Use your voice to nibble the words for flavor,
Each one you taste, is perfectly sweet,
For encouraging aspiring minds
To generate and rejuvenate
Learning in an astounding way,
Check out the stew often stirring and mixing
Poems and expressions together making sure
The words are tasteful and delightful,
Before you speak
Pull up a chair, sit right down
And serve your crew
A bowl of Inspirational Stew.

*Claritha D. Ingram*

## WITTY WISDOM

Preparing for a new horizon?
Proper preparation prepares
For future frolicking.
Pleasing personalities
Make
The jerky journey jovial.
Purpose propels perseverance.
Negative attitude alters altitude.
Scholars' self-indulgence strengthens
Success.
Redirect, rise up, refocus
And restore your vision
For future fulfillment.

*Claritha D. Ingram*

# THINK ABOUT IT

Butterflies come wrapped in cocoons,
Pearls come wrapped in oysters,
Young minds come wrapped in
Curiosity, love, wonderment, talent,
And fascinating, amazing abilities,
That's unbelievable.

Discover their exceptional, extraordinary
Distinctiveness then,
Drown their thoughts with
Information, wisdom and words of
Encouragement, after that,
Watch unique attributes
And possibilities unfold.

*Claritha D. Ingram*

# SPOKEN WORDS

Like a comet pulled from orbit
As it passes the sun,
Like driftwood being pulled by
The current at sea,
Who's to say, out of a
Voice wails reassuring words.
Pulled from the heart
Won't interlock emotions,
Directing thoughts to
Reminisce education's purpose
All because of spoken words.

Like a melody begets a pause,
Hearing the rhythm of a beat,
Like music's different instruments,
Combined make a symphony,
Who's to say, one spoken word or
Two, maybe three or four,
 Intermixed won't leave a handprint
On the heart and mind of scholars
To visualize widely probable aspirations,
All because of encouraging words.

Like the bright morning sun's glassy reflection
On the deep blue sea,
Like a rainbow's arch of colorful light
When raindrops mist,
Who's to say, uplifting words
Won't illuminate sparkling light,

Igniting endless curious productive doers,
To achieve great heights,
All because of inspiring words.

Like autumn leaves change colors
On a crispy cool fall day,
Like a chameleon's ability to change colors
According to variation in light
Who's to say, expressions of praise
Won't change attitudes of ingenious thinkers,
To envision capability of distant possibility
All because of reassuring words,
Spoken compassionately from the heart.

*Claritha D. Ingram*

# FROM A TEACHER TO STUDENTS

I can educate you but
I cannot make you appreciate the learning.
I can try to point you in the right direction but
I cannot be there to lead you.
I can grant you privileges but
I cannot account for them.
I can teach you right from wrong but
I cannot always decide for you.
I can teach you about kindness and
Compassion but
I cannot force you to be kind.
I can offer you advice but
I cannot force it upon you.
I can teach you to smile and how to make friends
But I cannot make you unselfish.
I can teach you to respect but
I cannot demand you to show honor.
I can teach you how to achieve excellence but
I cannot force it upon you.
I can advise you about character but
I cannot change you.
I can advise you about a good education but
I cannot force it upon you.
I can tell you about real life stories but
I can not change your attitude.
I can tell you how to avoid conflict but
I cannot protect you.
I can tell you about lofty goals but
I cannot achieve them for you.
I can teach you about obstruction but
I cannot dodge them for you.
It's your choice,
Your decision determines the outcome.

*Claritha D. Ingram*

# ARE YOU THINKING?

## WHEN YOU THINK ABOUT THE FUTURE, WHAT COMES TO MIND?

Do you think about the person
You want to be as an adult?

## THINK BIG!

Do you think about:
A person who establishes his or her own enterprise…
- The entrepreneur
- The inventor
- The doctor
- The lawyer
- The oceanographer
- The designer
- The engineer
- The architect
- The astronaut
- The sports analyst

A person who writes stories…
- The reporter
- The playwright
- The free-lancer

Imagine making a change someway, somehow, some place.

## WHILE GETTING AN EDUCATION, WHAT DO YOU THINK ABOUT?

Do you think about:
Being the kind of student that your parents
Will be proud of and brag about?

What about letting off a character light that reflects that "AHA" moment to astutely show a KEEN DEVELOPED MIND?

- ♦ A SCHOLAR...
  With unbelievable instincts and ability,
  Letting off a refined disposition.
- ♦ A LEARNER...
  Who always assumes responsibility,
  Honoring promises to education.
- ♦ AN HONOR STUDENT...
  Flourishing with high esteem, opening
  Pathways to reach far beyond expectations.
- ♦ A TRAIL BLAZER...
  Who takes steps to be transformed
  Into a respectable and accomplished scholar,
  Leaving a positive trail for others to follow.

**PRETTY AMAZING, DON'T YOU THINK?**

**WHEN YOU THINK ABOUT YOUR ATTRIBUTES, WHAT DO YOU THINK ABOUT?**

Do you think about:
- Respectful
- Kind
- Cooperative
- Responsible
- Smart
- Obedient
- Considerate
- Courageous
- Self-controlled
- Caring
- Committed
- Audacious

*Do you see those features making you a better student?*

# HOW CAN YOU BECOME A BETTER STUDENT?

## *Do you think:*
1. Sow seeds of knowledge every day.
2. Plan your course.
3. Immerse yourself into learning to
   Make knowledge yours to keep.
4. Study, focus, listen to maximize your learning.
5. Ask questions, be inquisitive.
   It's hard to fall down when you have
   Knowledge holding you up.
6. Exercise flawlessness, the collective beauty of this
   Will tell your scholastic story beautifully.
7. Show human kindness to inspire others through your
   Good manners, expressions, gestures and voice tone.

# WHAT'S ON YOUR AGENDA FOR THE FUTURE?

# ARE YOU THINKING?
## IF NOT, WHY NOT?

*Claritha D. Ingram*

# A VOICE THAT SINGS

Use your voice to sing,
There's no vocal coaching,
To go la, la, la,
There's no hip-hop for
Vocal rhyme,
There's no mellow sound
Of music playing,
No drums tapping rhythmically
To a beat;
The only tuneful melody
You hear
Are spoken words that flow from
A scholarly learner's voice,
Sharing knowledge, amplifying
Informational facts,
To deliver a memorable presentation.

That powerful vocal melody is a gift
Everyone possesses,
However, vocalization doesn't favor
Those who sit still quietly.
Blend your strongest, loudest sound
In collaboration with knowledge,
Let it sashay from your out-let pipes
Noting punctuation symbols
Arranging the rise and flow of
Vocal proficiency, expressing
That jazzy sound of knowledge.
Peers listen in amazement, emotions
Explode, hands clapping, heads moving,
Feet stumping;
An encore is called,
For that melodious sound of lyrics
And the voice that WOWED!

*Claritha D. Ingram*

# FOOD FOR THOUGHT

Knowledge does not just happen,
It imposes obligation
And responsibility;
Believe in you
But require more of you,
Highlight your purpose,
Your joy, your ambition;
You can't see the unseen,
Yet, possibility reveals
Dreams are achievable,
Signaling richly, rewarding opportunities.
Embrace the knowledge,
The moment is now,
Turn up the brilliance,
Absorb knowledge till the
Very last drop
And make each day of learning
A refreshing one;
Information gives rise to creativity,
And freedom of expression.

*WHAT'S ON YOUR AGENDA TODAY!*

*Claritha D. Ingram*

# INVISIBLE SHADOWS

HINDRANCES, invisible shadows
Roam into classrooms every day.
Undaunted by the lesson,
These wandering bodies,
Sometimes to the left or right,
Before or behind,
Yet, glancing out into this tidal wave
Of brilliant thinkers, I know
Those shadows won't stop YOU.

ROADBLOCKS, invisible shadows
Hang around classrooms every day.
On their daily prowl teaming up to
Cause havoc just to hold back aspiring
Champions' spirit to learn,
However, peering out into this ocean liner
Of eager learners in front of me,
I know the damaging interruption
Won't hinder YOU.

BLOCKADES, invisible shadows
Leisurely sit in classrooms every day.
Mingling with learners,
Blocking knowledge is their game,
Self-gratification is their aim.
Nevertheless, glancing out into this sea
Of ambitious minds, I know that commotion
Won't distract YOU.

HURDLES, invisible shadows
Tiptoe into classrooms every day.
Snoozing, staring, stretching, setting sights
On learning avoidance,
Yet, as I look out into this class of
Promising scholars,
I know the rudeness won't stop YOU.

UPROARS, invisible shadows
Creep into classrooms every day.
With their own agenda, unaware,
If one never dares to build their spaceship,
They will never launch the rocket
They are capable of building,
Nevertheless, as I observe the enthusiastic scholars
On this ocean cruiser,
I am sure the disorder won't
HOLD YOU BACK.

*Claritha D. Ingram*

## CREATIVE THINKING

**"I'M LEARNING FOR A PURPOSE WITH ANTICIPATION"**
A thought to think to yourself every day
Setting the mind in motion
To energize the passion to plunge into each
Assignment like a learning pioneer
In pursuit of a dream.

**"I'M LEARNING FOR A PURPOSE WITH A DREAM"**
Don't ever let the idea sleep,
Let it engulf your daily conversation
To spark that extraordinary flow of creativity
Driving the passion to achieve
Great things can be accomplished.

**"I'M LEARNING FOR A PURPOSE WITH HOPE"**
As the sun folds down behind the clouds
And dark night swoops into your room
Silence surrounds your thoughts
As you close your eyes, reflect
On a dream, a goal, a passion, with a possibility,
Freeze the thought, frame the thinking,

**"I'M LEARNING FOR A PURPOSE WITH A PASSION."**

*Claritha D. Ingram*

# TEACHING TIPS

1. Consistency is important. Build a visual memory of the poems by selecting one poem for focus during the week.

2. Let the children recite it daily as you navigate them through each verse.

3. Encourage them to chime in and be creative -- using expressive voices and gestures. This gives you an opportunity to make them feel good about themselves regardless of the obstacles faced in the classroom or in the community.

4. As a reminder, display the message -- poem, verse or saying -- somewhere so that it is readily available throughout the day.

5. In the case of a disciplinary issue, do not interrupt instruction. Instead, have the expressions available on note cards. Then, when students are playing around or ignoring the lesson, just walk and place a note on the desk that speaks to the inappropriate behavior. Again, do not interrupt instruction to handle a discipline problem. In my experience, after the note card is read, student attention is quickly recaptured as the student moves forward with the learning. After class or when students are working independently, those

students with cards are called to "the situation table" to discuss the problem. If the problem continues, a parent conference is called. Three or more note cards during a grading period will determine the conduct grade.

6. Set a positive tone for learning in your classroom by starting a child's day with words of encouragement. This stimulates the imagination, improves the ability to focus on the learning, helps them to relax, and takes their mind off outside problems.

7. Remember, the classroom is where children's dreams and teachers' expertise collide. When you strive to excite their hearts and reveal their genius, you will achieve it.

8. Parents and community helpers who work with children can use the poems and expressions to encourage a commitment to education.

9. Parents can select a poem or an expression that speaks to behavior, academic performance or just to boost their spirit every day and posting it in a visible location in the home.

10. For daily encouragement, parents can use a poem or a verse from the book -- even choose one of their own favorite poems -- to write confidence notes with words of praise and encouragement. The note would be a welcomed surprise placed in pocket, backpack, purse, lunch bag, pencil box or notebook.

# POEMS FOR THE HEARTS AND MINDS OF YOUNG SCHOLARS

# IT'S UP TO YOU

One song can spark a moment,
One flower can wake the dream.
One tree can start a forest,
One bird can herald spring.
One smile begins a friendship,
One handclasp lifts a soul.
One star can guide a ship at sea,
One word can frame the goal.
One vote can change a nation,
One sunbeam lights a room.
One candle wipes out darkness,
One laugh will conquer gloom.
One step must start each journey.
One word must start each prayer.
One hope will raise our spirits,
One touch can show you care.
One voice can speak with wisdom,
One heart can know what's true,
One life can make the difference,
You see, *it's up to you!*

*Author Unknown*

# EVERYONE CAN'T BE IN THE FRONT ROW

Life is a theater, invite your audience carefully. Not everyone is healthy enough to have a front row seat in our lives. There are some people in your life that need to be a friend from a distance. It's amazing what you can accomplish when you let go, or at least minimize your time with draining, negative, incompatible, not-going-anywhere people or friendships.

Observe the friends and people around you. Pay attention. Which ones lift and which ones lean? Which ones encourage and which ones discourage? Which ones are on a path of growth uphill and which ones are going downhill? When you leave certain people or friends, do you feel better or feel worse? Which ones always criticize, or don't really understand, know or appreciate you?

The more you seek quality, respect, growth, peace of mind, love and truth around you, the easier it will become for you to decide who gets to sit in the front row and who should be moved to the balcony of your life. You cannot change the people around you. But you can change the people you are around.

*Author Unknown*

■

"**If you don't like something, change it.
If you can't change it, change your attitude.
Don't complain.**" (*Maya Angelou*)

# SCORING

You can touchdown or fumble,
Be defeated or win the set,
Shoot a field goal or miss your shot,
Hit a homerun or strike out,
Run to cross the finish line
Or quit the race.

Don't spend your time running up and down
The education field yard and
Never scoring; have an objective, a goal,
And make it happen.
Take every drop of courage,
Every ounce of determination,
Every minute of existing knowledge,
And tower above proficiency.

Tackle challenges,
Take on competitive risks,
Then slam dunk the knowledge
To score big time.
It all starts with an N.B.A. scholar,
A Natural Born Achiever,
And I guess that's you!

*Claritha D. Ingram*

# CONFIDENT

It's time to build CONFIDENCE,
    Believe in yourself,
        Build on it,
            Radiate it,
                And finally,
Come into your own.
                      When you believe in
                Your ability, you can
        Accomplish great things.

There's a BIG, BIG WORLD
    Out there,
        A BIG, BIG FIELD
            Of hope, opportunity and excitement
        Awaits those who have the
        WILLPOWER and
COURAGE
        To work hard to achieve your goal.

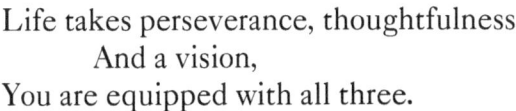

Life takes perseverance, thoughtfulness,
    And a vision,
You are equipped with all three.

You can help to show those attributes
By finding that button inside you
Then push it
LIKE CRAZY!!!
Reinforce your commitment and believe in YOU!!!
ARE YOU READY?

HERE WE GO...

* Let your attitude show your strength.
* You must blow your own horn.
* Find your inner light and let it shine, shine, shine.
* Do something bold.
* Find your STRONGEST attribute and let it be a surprise.

The more you project your strength,
>   The more powerful you will become,
>> IT TAKES CONFIDENCE!!!

*Claritha D. Ingram*

# THE BUZZ

Love learning
Be curious
Be extraordinary
Be flexible
Be prepared
Be excited
Have an interested mind
Rack up challenges
Explore, read, study
Generate ideas
Follow your interest
Build on your strength
Come with overflowing ideas
Elaborate, correct, erase, perfect
Own responsibility
Find your intellectual button
Demonstrate persistence
Do, dream, dare
Be tenacious, unrelenting,
The most valuable tools
To bring education into light.

*Claritha D. Ingram*

## EDUCATION IS ...

Education Is Opportunity ... Take Advantage Of It.
Education Is A Journey ... Continue It.
Education Is Knowledge ... Grasp It.
Education Is Irreplaceable ... Embrace It.
Education Is A Gift ... Receive It.
Education Is Very Valuable ... Don't Waste It.
Education Is Awesome ... Enjoy It.
Education Is A Melody ... Sing It.
Education Is A Seed, It Keeps Growing ... Plant It.
Education Speaks To Opportunity ... Believe It.
Education Is Your Bridge Of Hope ... Build It.

*Claritha D. Ingram*

# DELIGHT YOURSELF

Delight yourself to a wonderful treat
Everyday you walk into a classroom,
Dive into the books.
Melt into the knowledge
And enjoy the pleasantness of learning
Like it's...
The New York cheesecake
Dripping with strawberries,
The cream puff in a Twinkie,
The icing inside the Oreo cookie,
The caramel kisses filled with nuts,
The candy on a delicious candy apple,
Then press on to obtain
All of the deliciousness
Out of learning.
Schooling deliciously directs you
Toward self-independence, self-belief,
And self-trust.

*Claritha D. Ingram*

# WHAT IS KNOWLEDGE?

KNOWLEDGE, is a brainy food sprinkled
With anticipation,
KNOWLEDGE, is that small window of hope
To elevate your game to another level,
KNOWLEDGE, is your ticket, your rock, your gem
For upward mobility,
KNOWLEDGE, is that worldly glass door for imaginations,
To visualize and dream big,
KNOWLEDGE, is an incredibly powerful force that
Dominates a classroom,
KNOWLEDGE, is your fabric for you to weave the ordinary
Into exceptional,
KNOWLEDGE, is your blueprint to prepare you
For that golden period of adulthood,
KNOWLEDGE, prepares aspiring young minds to be
Valuable contributors, to our workforce and society,
KNOWLEDGE, is a source of information, for opportunity,
KNOWLEDGE, awakens and intensifies the mind and
Heart to be the best,
KNOWLEDGE, possesses greater power
Of flexibility
KNOWLEDGE, is a gift filled with possibilities,
KNOWLEDGE, is your x-factor to exemplify
The best of the best,
KNOWLEDGE, is unbelievable, don't ever
Underestimate its power,
The good news is, the cost is cheap,
All you pay is time and attention,
I re-kə-mend you take advantage of all
KNOWLEDGE has to offer and more.

*Claritha D. Ingram*

# PRESS FORWARD

Sitting on the sideline
Blindsided by distractions
An outsider observing,
Nose pressed against the glass,
Observing peers actively engaged
Gaining knowledge, receiving essential
Information, becoming more astute,
If you fail to embrace champions
Of progress you miss out on
An important opportunity
To secure a good education for the future,
Where you are now is not a permanent stand,
Let transformation take place
Any moment can be a moment to start,
Plant your feet firmly today,
Cast your eyes toward tomorrow.

*Claritha D. Ingram*

# IT'S YOUR FAULT

You can't get a job because
You don't have A HIGH SCHOOL DIPLOMA.

YOU DON'T HAVE A DIPLOMA
BECAUSE YOU DIDN'T PASS THE TEST.

YOU DIDN'T PASS THE TEST
BECAUSE YOU DID NOT FULFILL
YOUR RESPONSIBILITY.

YOU DID NOT ASSUME YOUR RESPONSIBILITY
BECAUSE YOU FAILED TO LISTEN.

YOU failed to LISTEN
BECAUSE YOUR ATTITUDE GUIDED YOUR ACTIONS.

YOUR ACTIONS DETERMINE YOUR SUCCESS,
Your success depends on your skills.

YOUR SKILLS depend on knowledge,
Knowledge influences thinking.
YOU CONTROL,
YOU COMMAND,
YOU DIRECT,
YOU DECIDE,
YOU CONCLUDE,
Your failure is your fault.

*Claritha D. Ingram*

# DREAMS

Are you dreaming, or acting on a dream?
It's not about having dreams,
It's about achieving,
Dreaming is easy,
Acting on a dream takes
A course of action,
As it is revealed, it all starts with,
Aspiration, purpose, self-confidence and,
Willpower, even audacity,
Saying to yourself, "Hey, wait a minute,
I want this, or I want that,"
Are just words, think about it,
Employment, currency, shelter, mobility
Grow out of a dream,
Then pushing the boundaries,
Chipping away at the books,
Every minute, every hour, every second
Of the day to
Accomplish your fixed goal,
That's the power of a dream.

*Claritha D. Ingram*

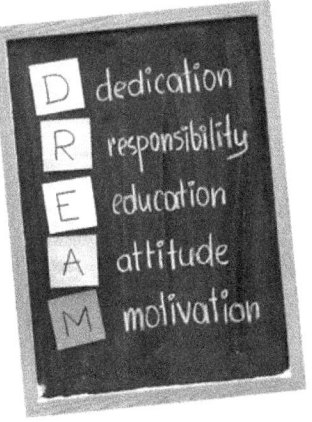

# CHANGE

I am changing,
I am releasing the negatives,
Letting them blow pass,
Like a breeze,
Ripping falling leaves
From an old oak tree.
All my old habits
Will be hard to let go of
What I thought to myself
Was having fun
When I was in Kindergarten and
First Grade and Second and Third,
Even Fourth maybe, but
I'm older now,
Thinking about my future
And I am changing,
What never occurred to me
What I thought was amusing
Was an ultimate intervention
And did not support my
Dream or vision.

*Claritha D. Ingram*

# THINK

You are intelligent, why not show it,
You can steer yourself in any direction you choose,
Why not walk a straight path,
Take time to think beyond the ordinary,
Before you step left, before you step right,
Move forward, or backward,
Consider the pros and cons,
Making the right choice today,
Can surely impact life greatly tomorrow.

Obstacles will surely cross your path,
Dilemmas will entice you,
When you come to the flashing light,
The answer lies within your
Head and heart, don't take a risk
And close the door on opportunity,
You better think before you step left,
Before you step right, move forward,
Or backward, making the wrong choice today,
Can surely impact life greatly tomorrow.

Contemplating on what to do
Is a distraction, consider consequences,
Great minds think for themselves,
Declare today to never be misled or deceived
Wake up to high expectation
You better think before you step left,
Before you step right, move forward or backward,

Making the wrong choice today,
Can surely impact life greatly tomorrow.

Don't lose focus on what's ahead tomorrow,
You have a plan and if your plan fails you fail,
Think like a champion, reveal your intelligence,
Making the right choices grows with
The ability to say, "No, that's not for me."
When that becomes crystal clear,
Doing the right thing becomes easy,
You better think long and hard,
Before you step left, before you step right,
Move forward, or backward,
Making the wrong choice today,
Can surely impact life greatly tomorrow.

*Claritha D. Ingram*

## RULES AND PROCEDURES

I demand only the best
Of what life has to offer,
Rules and procedures
Are expected,
I like the feeling that
You can't get away with anything,
This makes me immensely hopeful,
My approach to rules and procedures
Is not an arbitrary list of do's and don'ts,
The belt of truth is
Dignity and self-worth are recognizable
In part on the strength of
Rules and procedures.

*Claritha D. Ingram*

# GATEWAY TO SUCCESS

**FORTUNATE** is the child
Whose memory card is ready
And knows the advantage of education,
Its true benefits.
**UNFORTUNATE** is the child not touched by
An aura of rich educational experiences,
Ignoring all academic learning seasoned with
Words of wisdom and encouragement.
**UNLUCKY** is the child
Falling into that trap of failure,
Pushing all dreams and ideas back
On the back burner,
No soaring, no hoping, and letting all ambitions die.
**FORTUNATE** is the child who
Plunges into learning seeking knowledge
In pursuit of a dream,
Victoriousness is recognized,
An honor of distinction is granted,
After that you are ready for the challenge,
That's the sign of **VICTORY!!!**

*Claritha D. Ingram*

# A PATHWAY TO NOWHERE

Are you engaging in conduct daily,
With no educational purpose,
Or benefit due to habitual behaviors,
That disregard realistic powers of knowledge?
Psyching oneself out of trying,
Expressing denial of self-control,
Abandoning respect for others,
Disregarding all rules of conduct,
You are traveling a path to NOWHERE!!!

Facets to delay learning while pursuing
Scholastic skills...
Are you an aspiring BASKETBALL PLAYER... always
Tossing paper across the classroom
Into the trash, flaunting your skill?
A disturbance to avoid learning,
You are traveling a path to NOWHERE!!!

What about the BEGGING MOOCHER... always
Borrowing educational tools
For learning, an annoyance to delay learning,
You are traveling a path to NOWHERE!!!

Now here comes the WANNABE MODEL... always
Flaunting her talent strolling back and forth
To the pencil sharpener, a distraction to interrupt learning,
You are traveling a path to NOWHERE!!!

Maybe you are the RISING REPORTER... always
Writing humiliating notes, spreading gossip,
Bullying, causing a commotion,
A digression to hold up the learning,
You are traveling a path to NOWHERE!!!

Are you the BUZZ-Z-Z-Z-Z-ING BROADCASTER... always
Chitchatting with any ear that will listen,
An annoying classroom interruption,
You are traveling a path to NOWHERE!!!

Are you the BUBBLING, BOUNCING COMEDIAN...
Always, without hesitation,
Jumping up and down, clowning around,
Using humor to deflect the learning,
You are traveling a path to NOWHERE!!!

There's a whole lot of happy in learning,
Flip the switch, bond with knowledge,
Despite daunting challenges,
Triumph comes from
Ingenuity, tenacity, audacity,
And a fierce, unflagging determination,
Redouble your effort, and believe that
You can do anything you want to
If you try hard enough and at this point,
You'll be traveling the path to self-reliance.

*Claritha D. Ingram*

# A POWERFUL TOOL

Perched above the neck beneath the skull
Working in the control room,
A powerful tool rules the body,
Directing thinking, feeling, attitude;
It even gives energy to
The mind as you develop and grow
Your soundtrack to awaken the senses;
It's your life support machine
Without it one can not function,
Everyone has one;
It's your bubbling, blazing brain,
Feed it information, become intelligent;
If fed properly, you'll have
An ally forever.

*Claritha D. Ingram*

# PRICELESS GEM

In this world
Knowledge, I know, is meaningful,
It can be applied in
Many useful ways to make
Life work for me,
Sometimes the road gets
Rough or steep,
At times I don't think
I can make it to the finish line,
But I am determined,
Confidence comes from within,
The important thing
Is that, if
I take the collaborative, multidisciplinary approach
To unlock full potential, it helps to become
Socially, emotionally and academically successful,
Often, there are no street signs,
Which can leave one a little
Frustrated or feeling lost and
Confused along the way,
But I'm always reminded
"You can't leave knowledge out of your life,"
That's why I'm committed and determined to
Make it to the finish line,
"KNOWLEDGE,"
A priceless gem to have in my
Safe deposit box.

*Claritha D. Ingram*

# YOU ARE HISTORY IN THE MAKING

History can't be confined to the past,
History can be made every single day
By future leaders just like you
So take action now to ensure it happens.
Create your legacy buzz,
You are defined by what you pass on.

History is more than those in the past.
It's a movement, an act by certain individuals,
Who have the ability to make time stand still.
They can be young learners with ideas
Who aren't afraid to have their stories told,
It starts with the vision of scholars just like you.

Ordinary students can be transformed into heroes.
You must have the confidence to make it happen,
Let your genius be a reminder
That you are a forthcoming hero,
A legacy in the making.
Make a statement, highlight your genius,
Create a masterpiece,
Something memorable, outstanding, terrific.

So let this merely be a
Reminder that you are history in the making,
Stand tall at the front of your class,
Plant seeds of knowledge nudging others
To follow.
Your legacy can make you a giant.

*Claritha D. Ingram*

# REFLECTIONS

In your zealous pursuit of knowledge,
Scrapbook experiences
Wearing a tiny camera
With adjustable lens to capture
Movements, expressions,
Voice and performance,
To transmit full color images.

Document your experiences,
Indeed, you will see your self reflections,
Will they make you smile?
Will they make you frown?
Or will you rip into small tiny pieces
Each picture frame by frame?

Portraits in your portfolio can be top-notch,
It depends on your scholastic course of action
And how you run the education race.
To ensure the best close up,
Capture your best pose while investing quality time
On the education stage.

Bring together your best images,
Indeed, you'll see outstanding reflections,
A genius waiting to be cultivated,
A hero with hidden strengths and capability,
All in your scrapbook collection
Spreading a longest lasting smile
Upon your happy face.

*Claritha D. Ingram*

# I AM IN CHARGE

I am a visionary, exemplifying
Dignity and integrity,
Investing in what I want today
And what I want tomorrow.
I WANT it, I want to OWN it, I'll GO for it!
Then I'll step out in style
And won't be afraid to show it,
I am the genius of the knowledge file,
Extraordinarily gifted, full of potential,
I will find the confidence within and persevere,
I'll never settle for mediocrity.
Dreams are achievable,
Great things can happen,
I am in charge of my destiny.

*Claritha D. Ingram*

■

**"Start where you are, do what you can, use what you have."** *(Tennis legend Arthur Ashe)*

# AIM HIGH

To reach maximum potential,
Take a giant step forward,
The classroom is your venue,
Start the learning on a high note,
Popularize the room with fruitful information.
Create, elaborate, develop and learn,
Demonstrate, perform, arouse and excite,
Don't stop looking ahead,
The world requires big picture thinking,
Think BIG!!!

**PAINT SWEEPING, COLORFUL, BROAD STROKES OF YOUR DREAM.**

*Claritha D. Ingram*

# ATTITUDE

Attitude, an internal mechanism
That gives off an awesome display of feeling,
The way of thinking, manners and mindset,
You control the way it flows:
Grip it if giving off glowing character light,
Rip it if giving off dim negative light.

A negative attitude represents zero,
It freezes dreams, blurs vision,
Steals knowledge from the learner.
Drop the negative attitude;
You'll find nothing more liberating,
More fulfilling, more enlightening
Than losing the pessimistic attitude.

The negative attitude
Steals from you and wins,
Shift your attitude to gratitude.
Get focused, get pumped,
Unleash your best
And reflect on your
Success, ability, and character.
Your attitude is defined by YOU!!!

*Claritha D. Ingram*

# MANAGE YOUR EDUCATION

Consider education as opportunity
For the future,
Expectations are high
But no dream is too large,
Planning helps to direct the path,
Put restrictions around obstacles,
Rearrange priorities and
Enjoy the pleasantness of learning.

Don't do bare minimum
When required to perform,
Take on challenges and
Exert one's self due to brilliance,
Confidence and inner strength,
Turn doubts into determination,
Excuses into excellence,
"I Can't" into "I Can", and
"So-So" into "SPECTACULAR!"

You have choices and possibilities
To help make changes in the world,
To make a difference,
Education and learning is
Your strength to stand up
Against competition,
If you honor your commitment,
It's not complicated, JUST DO IT!

*Claritha D. Ingram*

# FIND YOUR LIGHT

Life is a museum,
Consider your work
A candidate of interest,
Fan the flame,
Consider the idea,
Let it be bold,
Imagine probability,
And go for it,
The rest clicks easily,
Into place.
Stay relevant to learning,
Giving it 100%
Be enthusiastically driven,
Remain committed,
Victory will propel.
Your scientific invention,
Design, painting, print, voice
Need to be upon the
Museum wall of life,
A memory for a lifetime.

*Claritha D. Ingram*

# DOOR OF OPPORTUNITY

Success comes when doing things
The right way.
Find yourself
At the center of
OPPORTUNITY,
Build a house of knowledge first,
Serving as a starting point,
That's where basic academic skills meet,
The foundation is positioned,
Knowledge learned and understood
Can be recognized and the walls
Of higher education open doors to you,
Colleges, universities, trade schools
Dynamic places to be,
Thrust yourself at the center of, surprisingly,
Transformation.
Take time to study ... you become your own teacher.
Take time to think ... it's an amazing opportunity to
Manipulate thoughts.
Take time to appreciate wisdom ... it hitches the mind to
The beauty and good within.
Take time to silence the voice ... "I can't" -- and keep
Trying.
The door of opportunity will open
Without a strain.

*Claritha D. Ingram*

# SELF-PROMOTION

Self-pride speaks volume about
My moral fiber and plays
A major role in how society
Values my worth,
I carry it daily in my emotional tool box
And tackle it with determination,
Assuming responsibility,
Communicating knowledge,
To unlock full potential
Loving myself is the turning point,
For change,
Wrapping my thinking around
SELF-PRIDE, MY
ROCK, MY BADGE OF HONOR
SYMBOLIZING SELF-CONTROL, SELF-RESPECT,
SELF-WORTH, SELF-MOTIVATION,
I WEAR IT PROUDLY EVERYDAY.

*Claritha D. Ingram*

## YOU WANT POWER?

Power is the ability to shine your light on the world,
GREATNESS is seeing that light
Reflected back from the world,
With a good education imparting your genius
THE GREATEST USE OF POWER is the choice to share
Your smarts so that everyone else walks away illuminated
With a sense of their ability.
LET YOUR GENIUS SHINE and keep on shining on
Until the world sees your POWER.

*Author Unknown*

# DIRECT YOUR FUTURE

My journey begins at a very early age,
I step out to start a new
Lease on life,
My beautiful is finding my gift within,
Flaunt my genius
Own my talent, make history my way,
The result:
A visionary scholar, that embodies
Beautiful inside and out,
Drawing on rich knowledge that
Exemplifies possibility when you
Play by the rules.
Talented. Imaginative. Triumphant. Beautiful.
That's ME!!!

*Claritha D. Ingram*

# CONFESSION

I'm the boss of my life,
The Chief Life Officer,
I control everything
And that's why I understand that
My education is the catalyst
For economic opportunity
For my future,
The inner-self I will embrace
To clear the pathway for possibility,
Knowledge, my smart phone,
The instrument to make it happen
Eventually, and perhaps ultimately,
I am going to make it,
Not a wish.  A promise.
I can make it happen for me.

*Claritha D. Ingram*

# IF

If you can keep your head when all about you
Are losing theirs and blaming it on you,
If you can trust yourself when all men doubt you,
But make allowance for their doubting too;
If you can wait and not be tired by waiting,
Or being lied about, don't deal in lies,
Or being hated, don't give way to hating,
And yet don't look too good, nor talk too wise:

If you can dream – and not make dreams your master;
If you can think – and not make thoughts your aim,
If you can meet with Triumph and Disaster
And treat those two impostors just the same;
If you can bear to hear the truth you've spoken
Twisted by knaves to make a trap for fools,
Or watch the things you gave your life to, broken,
And stoop and build 'em up with worn-out tools:

If you can make one heap of all your winnings
And risk it on one turn of pitch-and-toss,
And lose, and start again at your beginnings
And never breathe a word about your loss;
If you can force your heart and nerve and sinew
To serve your turn long after they are gone,
And so hold on when there is nothing in you
Except the Will which says to them: "Hold on!"

If you can talk with crowds and keep your virtue,
Or walk with Kings – nor lose the common touch,
If neither foes nor loving friends can hurt you,
If all men count with you, but none too much;
If you can fill the unforgiving minute
With sixty seconds worth of distance run,
Yours is the Earth and everything that's in it,
And – which is more – you'll be a Man, my son!

*~ Rudyard Kipling*

# HOLD FAST TO DREAMS

Hold fast to dreams
For if dreams die
Life is a broken-winged bird
That cannot fly.
Hold fast to dreams
For when dreams go
Life is a barren field
Frozen with snow.

*~ Langston Hughes*

# MY PEOPLE

The night is beautiful,
So the faces of my people.

The stars are beautiful,
So the eyes of my people.

Beautiful, also, is the sun,
Beautiful, also, are the souls of my people.

*~ Langston Hughes*

# BOOK POWER

Find your brilliance in a book
Comprehensive information is powerful
Giving you a voice and
In that voice lies strength,
Generating an amazing discussion.
Let your intellectual capability move you
And find your voice in reading.

Learner's smart eventually emerges
Sharing reflective book chats,
Like a symphony your voice amplifies
And modulates into different genres
Giving out far-reaching information
Destined to build imaginations to dream.

Soon it becomes crystal clear
Knowledge hinges on information,
Information hinges on reading,
Reading hinges on books.
Sink into a squishy, mushy pillow
Relax and enjoy a good book.

*Claritha D. Ingram*

# PROMOTE YOURSELF, BE YOUR OWN PORTFOLIO AND RESUME, BLOW YOUR OWN HORN

When I make my grand entrance into a crowded place
I try to greet everyone with a smile on my face
But there is always someone who won't smile back
Because, they're too busy trying to make a wise crack
About a single little strand of hair that might be out of place
Or a spot of make-up that might show on my face
But, these kinds of people don't make me feel weak
I keep right on strutting and turn the other cheek….
I am proud of what I have to show
I walk with pride and let my qualities glow
I know some of us walk around with our heads
All up in the air
While those who envy us are always there to stare
It's just that we show our self-appreciation
Straight forward and out loud
I'm amazed that I can stand on my own two feet
And not ashamed around the people I meet
I know that I have style and grace that are known
No one can possess since it's my very own.
You too have a style that only you have the
Power to express
Your method of doing things only you possess
So, the very next time someone makes an
Insulting remark
To try and make you feel weak
Remember my motto keep right on
Strutting and
And turn the other cheek…

*Anonymous*

# THE BEST YOU CAN BE

Everyday there is a new opportunity.
Everyday there is a blank page.
Everyday you have a chance
To leave your mark.

No false moves.
No false starts.
No false promises.

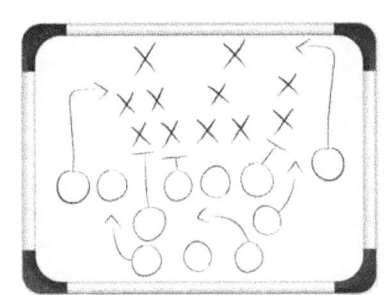

Don't let anything
Slow you down.

Don't let anything
Get in your way.

Don't let anything
Stop you.

Everybody needs something they can reach for and rely on.
Setting goals, then setting out to reach those goals is
Worth working hard for everyday. Your harvest comes at the end of
Your hard work. The results will be somewhere between
**OUTSTANDING** and **UNBELIEVABLE!!**

**OBSTACLES** do not exist.
**IMPOSSIBLE** is just a thought.
**I CAN'T** is not part of your vocabulary.

Compromise is not on your schedule.
    **Failure** is not part of your game plan.
    **Good enough** will never be able to hang with great.
If you are willing and your mind is open, knowledge will always
Find its way in. And you will never reach for anything less than
Great.

*Claritha D. Ingram*

## SPECIAL

I am special,

I represent the fabric of our future

Running wild in the wind.

I am truly a gentle spirit

Of the classroom

And create a passion

In those who are dedicated and

Fortunate enough to

Work with me.

*Claritha D. Ingram*

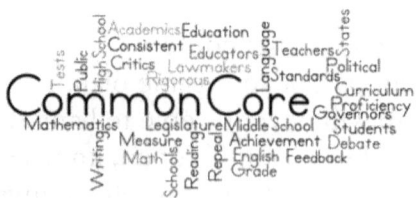

# THE CLASSROOM

A wealth of knowledge
Stacked all around you
Each day you drift through the door of learning
Keep high aspirations, not just because you are stirred,
But because you must to keep up with everyday curiosities,
A classroom is where it all happens
The true melting pot for learning,

An assortment of knowledge
Opens up to you each day you walk through
The door of learning,
You have a caring heart, a hidden genius, a mind willing,
Open your eyes to see, your ears to listen,
Your mind to achieve,
Excellence comes wrapped, draped and concealed
In confidence and certainty,
A classroom is where it all happens
The true melting pot for learning,

A classroom is steeped with information
Each day you enter for learning,
Be smart, be wise, aim high,
Surf the books for knowledge
Then share your creative thoughts
Tomorrow's greatness begins with you,
A classroom is where it all happens
The true melting pot for learning,

A classroom is where it all happens
The true melting pot for learning,
Take advantage of each proud accomplishment,
Capture your feelings
Hold on to those moments,
A classroom is where it all happens
The true melting pot for learning.

*Claritha D. Ingram*

# POSSIBILITY

**It's possible**
To sit quietly in a classroom and see success,
**It's possible**
To read books and see hope,
**It's possible**
To deliver excellence,
**It's possible**
To believe an education gives access to
A domain you can use for a lifetime,
**It's possible**
To look beyond high school and see higher education
**It's possible**
To see education as the hammer to shape the future,
**It's possible**
To deal with the adversity of following rules
And obey,
**It's possible**
Not to feed into anger, use logic and back away,

If you ponder all the possibilities
They lead to one conclusion, without a doubt,
Self-confidence turns possibilities into reality if you
Believe.

*Claritha D. Ingram*

# WHY AM I HERE?

I arrived early today
Before my peers
Before my teacher.
I want to be first in my seat today
Before the lights come on
Before instruction begins
I want to sit, relax, and reflect
I want to clear the cobwebs
And not lose focus of why
I am here today
I want to spend this day and
The days forthcoming
Taking advantage of my education
Without interference
I'm learning not because I have to
But because I want to.

I want to be considerate of others
As knowledge flows through the classroom
Taking steps to improve myself
It's the benefit of self-improvement, to
Improve me.
All I am saying is I want to change and renew my
Membership in this class today
Letting my new ambitious attitude
Captivate and inspire others to
Strive for excellence too.

*Claritha D. Ingram*

# WHAT'S BLOCKING THE LEARNING?

I want to learn,
What's blocking the learning?

I want to be more attentive,
What's blocking the vision?

I want to enjoy learning,
What's blocking the feeling?

I want to be an achiever with the
Best disposition,
What's blocking the person?

I want to be a productive citizen
Not a liability,
What's blocking the process?

I want to make my parents proud!
What blocking the performance?

Of all the things I want,
As thoughts snap inside my head,
Is freedom of flexibility
To be the best that I can be,
What's blocking my way?

*Claritha D. Ingram*

## GUIDANCE

Instruct me to open a book
I see words,
Guide me carefully through the literature,
I will learn,
Tell me about knowledge, I'll give ear,
Educate me leaving a memorable
Imprint, I'll remember,
Require me to follow rules,
I'll hear you,
Explain carefully with encouraging words,
I'll adhere and obey,
Talk to me about character, I'll listen,
Coach me and paint a vivid picture,
I'll change,
With guidance and understanding,
I'll modify and improve,
Exemplifying the best of the best,
Don't sacrifice instruction,
Or discount ability,
Teach values, ignite dreams, and
Inspire hope,
The negative will turn into a positive.

*Claritha D. Ingram*

# WHAT IF

What if, I believe I am instrumental
In my success?
What if, I believe I can leap into knowledge with a
Dream and enjoy every delightful minute of learning?
What if, I believe I have the academic talent
To be whatever I want to be?
What if, I believe I can make a productive
Effort to achieve excellence?
What if, I believe I can cherish the idea
That knowledge rules long into the future?
What if, I believe I can let knowledge jell then
Come alive to empower my imagination to dream?
What if, I believe that education is
My passport to the future only if I have
The skills and knowledge to pursue my dreams?
What if, I believe I can embrace differences
And change the world?
What if, I believe that I will be there
To make sure it all happens for me?
I believe I am up for the challenge.

*Claritha D. Ingram*

# ALL ABOUT ME

All the knowledge I have inside
Has not been noticed yet.
I am kind of smart, brilliant, intelligent,
One might say,
But sometimes I feel unprepared, then
At times unchallenged, so I drift,
To show, I have a mind, heart, and soul within:
Imperfection vanishes, knowledge illuminates,
Attention recaptured.
Persistence pushes me with force,
But courage keeps me moving
And self-discipline keeps me grounded.
Learning information to help create the best
Experience for me to follow the path that calls me,
Will make me an incredible, smart scholar.

*Claritha D. Ingram*

 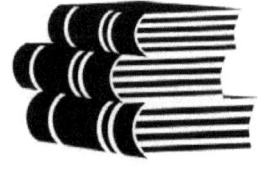

# MY PROFILE

I am INCREDIBLE
I am INSPIRED,
I am MARVELOUS,
I am SENSATIONAL,
I am utterly FABULOUS,
SUPER SMART and
TALENTED,
Glowing with
(WOW!)
SELF-ASSURANCE.

This symphony of words,
Wrapped around my thinking,
Is an ego-centric movement
To celebrate "me,"
As I am naturally,
Then serve to teachers
Appropriately.
How delightfully enjoyable that
Would be,
Every word served tells about ME.

*Claritha D. Ingram*

# I AM THE GREATEST

I am Fierce!
When I look into the sea of life
At my stunning reflection,
I see a scholar, strong, determined
To face education's challenges.

I am Triumphant!
When I look into the sea of life
At my lovely reflection,
I see a dreamer who sees no barriers,
No obstacles to stop the learning.

I am Radiant!
When I look into the sea of life
At my beautiful reflection,
I see a masterpiece working with a
Body of knowledge, ready to be challenged.

I am a well-rounded Scholar!
When I look into the sea of life
At my gorgeous reflection,
I see an achiever with drive, enthusiasm,
Ready to achieve.

I am Phenomenal!
When I look into the sea of life,
I see an ingenious thinker
Ready to eliminate obstacles,
Erase limitations
And accelerate excellence.

*Claritha D. Ingram*

## MAKE IT HAPPEN

I am weaving the fabric of excellence
Planting my feet, my mind, my heart
In the direction I want to go,
Employing passion, perseverance, precision,
Expectation, anticipation mounts
Driven by intellect, talent, and fortitude
Filling gaps with foundational skills,
To triumph when faced with adversity.

I'm weaving the fabric of excellence
Breaking through barriers,
Taking on challenges,
Broadening my knowledge base,
To define my destiny
I am unequivocally proud with gusto
And enthusiastically clear on my vision,
Understanding knowledge embodies
The need for success.

*Claritha D. Ingram*

# THE BUILDER

I am an architect,
Working inside those education walls
With an ambitious mind
Connecting to positive upbeat language,
Idleness sometimes enters the brainwave;
Positive wisdom strengthens and
Supports the unfilled hollow mind
Leaving no yawning gap between,
Challenge embraces,
Confidence sprouts,
Determination blooms,

Thoughts well occupied,
Mind working and working well
Connecting where knowledge dwells,
Intelligence entirely unpolluted,
Else life be incomplete.

Sitting inside those education walls,
A scholar eager to learn
With tiny feet walking the hallways,
With an open curious mind,
Calm and confident,
In all, I'm all fired up,
Ready to build learning.

*Claritha D. Ingram*

# LIFELONG LEARNER

A lifelong learner I am, I am,
Capable of achieving academic skills,
My voice harmonizes beautifully through
Spoken words, performance and pen,
Seeking perfection in whatever I do,
Open-mindedness combined with personality
And ability working together
Increasingly expand classroom experiences,
Eventually, brainpower explodes
Revealing beauty, and smarts within.

A code of ethics, explicit words of
Encouragement
Spark the desire for proficiency,
A clear understanding of expectation
Stimulates the desire to achieve,
Lured by determination
Words of assurance
Ignite the passion,
Which governs the attitude.

It's all about me, myself and I
Representing the breadth, and depth
Of a great mind that so eloquently
Symbolizes a scholar on a
Mission to be the best
That I can be.

*Claritha D. Ingram*

# PASSIONATE

I am passionate about education,

I am focused on my ambition,

I am unwaveringly determined

To learn, create, be first and

Develop innovative ideas

That will help me withstand

The next big thing that comes along.

I am looking for opportunity

To expand on infinite possibilities

So when my ability is measured,

It's measured of me,

Thanks to broadening

My knowledge base

That transformed me.

I am passionate about education.

*Claritha D. Ingram*

# INNER THOUGHTS

I envision myself
Ready to earn my degree,
Strolling across the graduation stage,
Wearing a black diamond-shaped hat
With a tassel turned to the side,
Showing a scholarly attitude,
Swirling, whirling, twiddling,
With excitement,
Dressed radiantly in self-confidence,
Glamorized in scholastic skills.
That's unbelievable, accepting
"MY VICTORY,"
Looking back in the rearview mirror,
Eavesdropping and listening eagerly
To loud applause, taking note
Of whispered words
I hear voices, saying
"EXCELLENCE DESERVES
RECOGNITION,
RECOGNITION DESERVES FRAMING."
Tomorrow will be your day.
What's your learning happy?

*Claritha D. Ingram*

## I AM READY

I am ready to elevate what I want and willing to
Work hard every day to achieve my goal.
I will adopt persistence,
I will adopt flexibility,
I will adopt superior goals,
I will adopt purpose,
I will adopt tough challenges,
I will adopt staying open to learning,
I will adopt avoiding conflicts,
I will adopt each one for the good.
What a delightful formula for a quality education!

*Claritha D. Ingram*

# WORD POWER

What shall I write?
What shall I say?
How shall I say it?
Stoke the fire
Expand your word appetite
READ, READ, READ,
Your rich word power will upsurge
Of all the things words can do tomorrow,
And, after that, for many tomorrows to come,
Form a delightful speech, an inspiring conversation,
A brief expression,
Maybe a promise, a pledge or
Just sharing awesome information,
Whatever the conversation, dialogue, exchange
Of words might be
Your tantalizing, eye-widening vocabulary
Will become the most captivating, interesting,
Thrillingest attention grabber one can
Possess, making you feel
Incredibly proud when you hear,
"Wow, what an astonishing, amazing vocabulary!"

*Claritha D. Ingram*

# MOVING FORWARD

Dancing to your own tune,
That's moving forward.
Learn by living, talking, listening,
That's moving forward.
Celebrating excellence,
That's moving forward.
Learning from mistakes,
That's moving forward.
Honoring your commitment,
That's moving forward.
Expressing yourself with
Pen, pencil, and voice,
That's moving forward.
Dream, wish, hope, soar,
That's moving forward.
Leaving your footprint
for others to follow,
That's moving forward.
Win national recognition
And set records,
That's moving forward.
Keep moving forward
Long enough and
When you look back you
Won't see mistakes,
That's moving forward.

*Claritha D. Ingram*

# SIGNIFICANT

### MY COMPETENCE,
Ingenious, showing my intelligence.

### MY PASSION,
Enthusiastic, excited about my work.

### MY IMAGINATION,
Clever, great ideas, skilled at
Creating, inventing, discovering.

### MY VISION,
Transformative, always open for change.

### MY DETERMINATION,
Unwavering, forever ready to learn new information,
Improving overall well-being.

*Claritha D. Ingram*

# I GOT THIS

I realize I can choose to rise like a phoenix
With knowledge power under my wings
The sky is the limit.
I go to sleep each night feeling fantastic
Realizing knowledge greatness
Is not crafted by sitting idly.
I am confident that
I can be my best self every day
Knowing I have emerged from the
Shadow of the classroom.
My imagination is so full of
Creative thoughts, there is no room
For negative reflection.
I've got better things in my imagination
Than to think about nit-picking.
I promise to treat myself
And others well along with
Building my confidence and stamina
For my overall education,
It is obvious I love myself,
I adore who I am.

*Claritha D. Ingram*

Be Careful
How You Act
You Never
Know Who's
Watching

# A POSITIVE APPROACH

# TO

# CLASSROOM MANAGEMENT

# LITERARY GEMS, THOUGHTS TO PONDER, WORDS TO LIVE BY

*Next to the originator of a good sentence is the first quoter of it. Your thought is well illustrated when you beautify the language with a quotation from the choicest of literature.*
*~ Ralph Waldo Emerson*

Teachers, immerse yourself when reading the literary gems and points to ponder in this section. Take a moment and pause while children reflect on what is being said. This is definitely a sure-fire way to capture attention as they sink their thoughts into the message.

Text is more than just an association between wisdom and inspiration. It speaks to respect, honor, courage and character. It is also relevant and something children can bite and chew on for a long, long, long time.

This extensive collection of literary gems, thoughts to ponder, and words to live by illuminate the awareness needed to help enhance the moral fiber of young people.

Don't let one person put their opinion on the journey you choose to take. No one can tell you what you can be, only you have the power to decide that for yourself. Continue to pursue your dream until you see the door closing on you. It begins with confidence and assurance and ends with the same.

There are few guarantees in life. But, it is a guarantee that if you fail to obtain a good educational foundation, your boat will sink when you set out to sail on the sea of opportunity. Your education is the passage through which you must go to launch your large vessel.

*~ Claritha D. Ingram*

Your education is a voyage of discoveries, the journey can be rough, yet, as in business you work hard to reach the top. Life's good when you rise to reach your lofty goal and ends with that unmistakable feeling of success.

*~ Claritha D. Ingram*

No one takes a negative and frames it. The negative has to always be developed into a positive for framing. Capture your best pose by getting a good education.

*~ Claritha D. Ingram*

You think knowledge can't bring you happiness? Just in case learn all you can now so you can be prepared. It's nice to see a brilliant mind at work. That's exhilarating in itself.

*~ Claritha D. Ingram*

"I am only one
But I am One
I cannot do everything."
But I can try to do something.
What I can do, that I
Ought to do and what I
Ought to do, with the
Ability within me I will do.

*~ Adam Clayton Powell*
*(quoting and paraphrasing Edward Everett Hale)*


Information is powerful,
   Knowledge is how you receive it.
      That's what make the world go round,
         So why not let knowledge become
            One of your most cherished treasures.

*~ Claritha D. Ingram*


"Every tomorrow is a vision of hope", climb high, climb far
   Your goal, the sky,
      Your aim, the stars.
         Don't stop until you
            Reach your dream.

*~ Claritha D. Ingram*


Without structure, you have no understanding or inner power;
   without inner power you have no peace; and without peace
      where is your joy?

*~ Bhagavad Gita*

IMPOSSIBLE is just a big word thrown around by small people who find it easier to live in the world they've been given than to explore the power they really have to change it. IMPOSSIBLE is not a fact. It's opinion. IMPOSSIBLE is not a declaration. It's a dare. IMPOSSIBLE is potential. IMPOSSIBLE is temporary. IMPOSSIBLE IS NOTHING.

*~ Unknown*

You underestimate your own brain power when you sell yourself short and refuse to tackle challenges. Brilliance favors those who put forth an effort. To emerge triumphantly you must get more involved in the learning. The little word found at the beginning of triumph is "TRY."

*~ Author Unknown, Adapted by Claritha D. Ingram*

Believe that it is possible to climb high, then discover the steps it takes to lead you to great heights then start climbing so you can leave your footprints on the ladder for others to follow.

*~ Claritha D. Ingram*

You may be disappointed if you fail, but you are doomed if you don't try.

*~ Beverly Sills*

You cannot wait for inspiration you have to inspire yourself.

*~ Unknown*

You are young, gifted and talented.
If you are silent, you will be forgotten,
If you do not advance, you will fall back,
If you walk away from any challenge your
Self-esteem will be forever scarred,
And if you cease to grow, even a little
You will become smaller.
Reject the stationary position because it
Is always the beginning of the end.

~ Og Mandino

You are an apprentice doing the daily chores
That it will take for you to become the master
Someday. No matter who ignores you or won't
Allow you to compete with others you, just stay in
The race then everyone will clearly recognize
That you are in it to win it because you too would
Like to add to the good in the
World.

~ Claritha D. Ingram

The ladder of success is never crowded at the top.
Pursue your highest aspiration and by the power of your
Pursuit the door of hope will open without a strain.

Claritha D. Ingram

You are comfortable in your own skin because you
Are acquiring knowledge,
Which will give you the skills needed to stay ahead of
Your competitive opponents.
Mix the two ingredients together (knowledge + skill)
Now you have powerful scholastic skills and intelligence in your
Tool box to give your resume
Credibility and Clout.

~ *Claritha D. Ingram*


Although there are obstacles and barriers,
There is no limitation to what can be achieved
When you put your mind to it and expand knowledge.
That BIG, BIG THOUGHT, BIG, BIG DREAM,
BIG, BIG IDEA can be actualized if you have the
BIG, BIG DETERMINATION to
Cement new information into the mind everyday
To reach a distant goal to earn the currency
To take you places
You've never gone before.

~ *Claritha D. Ingram*


Champions are made from something they have deep inside,
A desire, a dream, a vision. They have the stamina,
They have the skill and the will. But the will must be stronger
than the skill.

~ *Muhammad Ali*

Plant knowledge and knowledge will bloom;
Plant nothing and nothing will grow;
You can sow today, tomorrow will bring;
The blossom that proves what sort of thing;
Is the seed, the seed that you sow.

~ *Unknown*

The essence of learning isn't process but
Purpose...
Knowledge often occurs not because a
Person attempts to make a passing grade but
Because the person attempts to achieve a
Goal.

~ *Claritha D. Ingram*

Watch your thoughts, because they become words,
Watch your words, because they become actions,
Watch your actions, because they become your habits,
Watch your habits, because they become your character,
Watch your character, because it becomes your destiny.

~ *Unknown*

You never expect the unexpected until it happens
Always stay strong and never give up on yourself.

~ *Pam Thompson*

Life has to sometime turn you upside down before you can
Understand an education is what you need to prepare yourself
For the mainstream of life.

*~ Claritha D. Ingram*

You are never given a dream without also
Being given the ability to make it come true.
You have to make it happen. You can't just
Sit around and wait for it to come knocking
At your door. What you do today will
Determine what tomorrow will bring.

*~ Claritha D. Ingram*

There are three ingredients in life: Learning, Earning, Yearning.

*~ Unknown*

Only one person in the world can defeat you. That is yourself.

*~ Unknown*

Dreams come, dreams go, dreams take the mind on
A road to and fro. The high road, and the low,
And each of us must choose the way our lives should go.

*~ Das*

Be strong and dream the brightest, boldest thoughts and be
committed. Your commitment has to match your desire.

*~ Claritha D. Ingram*

Yesterday is gone, you cannot go back; tomorrow is yours and what you choose to do with it is all up to YOU.
*~ Claritha D. Ingram*

You were not born a winner, and you were not born a loser, you are what you make of yourself.
*~ Lou Holtz*

You are never really playing an opponent. You are playing yourself, your own highest standards, and when you reach your limits that is real joy.
*~ Arthur Ashe*

You must rouse into people's consciousness, your own prudence and strength, if you want to raise their character.
*~ Marquis de Vauvenargues*

You must begin to think of yourself as becoming the person you want to be.
*~ David Viscott*

Without hard work, nothing grows but weeds.
*~ Gordon B. Hinckley*

You can not build a dream on a foundation without knowledge; it will collapse under its own structure.
*~ Claritha D. Ingram*

Use your ability that has been given to you to make leaps and bounds and try to learn all you can to achieve excellence to be in a position to influence others. Perfect your talents and potentials to the ultimate.

~ *Denzel Washington*


There are no secrets to success: Don't waste time looking for them. Success is the result of perfection, hard work, learning from failure and loyalty to those for whom you respect.

~ *Gen. Colin Powell*


Life does not question what you know, or how you learn, only that you learn all you can while you can. Knowledge is your statement that shows the learning you receive.

~ *Claritha D. Ingram*


Discipline is the refining fire by which talent becomes ability.

~ *Roy L. Smith*

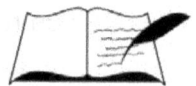

Never go out to meet trouble if you will just be still, nine times out of ten someone will intercept it before it reaches you.

·····

One reason folks get into trouble is that trouble usually starts out beginning with fun.

·····

When I want to speak, let me first think. Is it true? Is it kind? Is it necessary? If not, let it be left unsaid.

·····

People can be divided into three groups. Those who make things happen, those who watch things happen, and those who wonder what happened.

·····

Character is not an inheritance; each person must build it for himself.

·····

If you want to be successful, decide where you are going and start now. No race can be won until after the start has been made.

·····

Though we travel the world over to find the beautiful, we must carry it with us or we find it not.

~ *Emerson*

·····

"I am like that" does not help anything, "I can be different" does.

⌘

Life is like a mirror -- you get out of it what you put into it.

·····

A good listener is not only popular everywhere,
but, after awhile, he knows something.

*~ Wilson Minzer*

·····

Sometimes the thing you dread doing is the very thing you should do, just stop thinking about it and get busy.

·····

Every artist dips his brush into his own soul, and paints his own nature into his picture as he does in living his life.

*~ Henry Ward Beecher*

·····

The meaning of life is finding your gift;
the purpose of life is giving it away.

*~ Joy Golliver*

·····

The world makes way for the person who knows
where he is going.

*~ Emerson*

·····

Success is not measured by your victories, but by your recovery from your failures.

*~ Vic Preisser*

❖

The truth of the matter is that you always know the right thing to do. The hard part is doing it.

~ *Gen. H. Norman Schwarzkopf*

·····

Success in life isn't given; it costs attitude, ambition and acceptance.

~ *Jennifer Leigh Youngs*

·····

Our life is like a piece of paper on which every passerby leaves a mark.

~ *Ancient Chinese Proverb*

·····

Sometimes it's not anything your friend does that irritates you. It's just that you are spending way too much time together. You're too close for comfort! Maybe you need to branch out and seriously expand your friend base.

~ *Rukshan Mistry*

·····

Jealousy is a sign of insecurity, and it brings out the best in everyone. When insults are flying, stay safe by clamming up and fading into the background. Taking sides will lure you into the mess, and you could lose one or both of your friends! If it gets too stressful, go out with a happier crowd.

~ *Rukshan Mistry*

Vision, conviction and courage make the difference in living a successful life.
~ *Patricia A. Kornegay*

.....

We all have the power to choose our destiny.
~ *Patricia A. Kornegay*

.....

You must begin to think of yourself as becoming the person you want to be.
~ *David Viscott*

.....

Your imagination is your preview of life's coming attractions.
~ *Albert Einstein*

.....

Your goals are the road map that guide you and show you what's possible for life.
~ *Les Brown*

.....

Your chances of success in any undertaking can always be measured by your belief in yourself.
~ *Robert Collier*

.....

You've got to follow your passion. You've got to figure out what it is you love -- who you really are. And have the courage to do that. I believe that the only courage anyone ever needs is the courage to follow your own dreams.
~ *Oprah Winfrey*

★

When your dream dies, don't bury it, respect it and keep on dreaming. You were born to stand out.

*~ Unknown*

·····

Education inspires much wanderlust, a lot of hard work and very little play.

*~ Anonymous*

·····

Doing the best at this moment puts you in the best place for the next moment.

*~ Oprah Winfrey*

·····

Learn from mistakes of others, you can't live long enough to make them all yourself.

*~ Eleanor Roosevelt*

·····

The days come and go but they say nothing, and if we do not use the gifts they bring, they carry them as silently away.

*~ Benjamin E. Mays*

·····

Time is neutral and does not change things. With courage and initiative, leaders change things.

*~ Jesse Jackson*

Your mind is like a creative medium so you serve yourself with superior thoughts, and place yourself in a position to be the best. The best coach with the strongest power over performance is the coach that lives in you.

~ *Keith Harrell*

·····

Make each day useful and cheerful and prove that you know the worth of time by employing it well. Then youth will be happy, old age without regret, and life a beautiful success.

~ *Louisa May Alcott*

·····

You had better live your best and act your best and think your best today; for today is the sure preparation for tomorrow and all the other tomorrows that follow.

~ *Harriet Martineau*

·····

Quitting is not an option when there are possibilities. Always have the courage to try.

~ *Jane Emanuel*

·····

Of all the unhappy people in the world, the unhappiest are those who have not found something they want to do.

~ *Unknown*

♥

The greatest essentials of happiness are something to do, something to love, and something to hope for. Trouble is usually produced by those who don't produce anything except trouble.

*~ Unknown*

·····

If a man empties his purse into his head, no man can take it away from him. An investment in knowledge always pays the best interest.

*~ Benjamin Franklin*

·····

He who starts behind in a great race of life must forever remain behind or run faster than the man in front.

*~ Benjamin E. Mays*

·····

It's a joy to have people look at you and see knowledge, character and intelligence.

*~ Anonymous*

·····

Knowledge has no borders. If your mind is not open to absorb knowledge then keep your mouth shut.

*~ Anonymous*

↗

Imagination allows one to soar, while laziness consents to creep.
One can not consent to creep when one has the ability to soar.

~ *Anonymous*

## CARING RAP

A friend is what we want to be,
We'll treat each other respectfully,
We can help each other grow and learn,
Caring, sharing, it will show,
Differences develop us -- not divide
Making us stronger, side by side

You be you and I'll be me,
Together we'll get along intelligently
Because we are all friends
And part of a family

~ *Anonymous*

·····

Seek first to understand and then to be understood. You do not listen with the intent to understand; you listen with the intent to reply. You filter everything through your own opinion.
The greatest thing you can do is surprise yourself; listen and think first then reply.

~ *Anonymous*

Failure is not a permanent condition. It only strengthens determination and fuels the desire to succeed.

~ *Anonymous*

·····

Our doubts are traitors, and make us lose the good we oft might win, by fearing to attempt.

~ *William Shakespeare*

·····

It is how you feel about yourself throughout the day that gives The tone, the texture, and the quality to life itself.

~ *Unknown*

·····

The highest reward for man's toil is not what he gets for it but what he becomes by it.

~ *Unknown*

·····

Doing the best you can with the opportunities that come along, will get you further than idly wishing for the big chance that may never arrive. Whatever impedes a man but doesn't stop him aids his progress.

~ *Unknown*

·····

There is no limit to what you can accomplish when you develop the mind and use books to acquire knowledge.

~ *Dr. Ben Carson*

The firefly only shines when on the wings; so it is with the mind; when once you rest, we darken.

~ *Philip James Bailey*

·····

Treat yourself like a work of art, your action frames your character, your character mirrors your personality. Frame yourself appropriately for adulthood.

~ *Claritha D. Ingram*

·····

Always have the courage to try. You never expect the unexpected until it happens. But stay strong and don't ever give up on yourself. Never stop trying.

~ *Pam Thompson*

If opportunity doesn't knock, you have not put in a door.

~ *Pam Thompson*

·····

There is always someone around to help you, you just have to look in the right places then ask for help.

~ *Margaret Morehead*

·····

It's your right to care nothing about yourself, but you must be willing to accept the consequences for the failure, and you must never think that those who have chosen to work, while you played, rested, and slept, will share their bounties with you.

~ *Marva Collins*

Your success and education can be companions that no misfortune can depress, no crime can destroy and no enemy can alienate. Without education, man is a slave, a savage wandering from here to there believing whatever he is told.
~ *Marva Collins*

·····

Time and chance come to us all, you can be either hesitant or courageous. You can swiftly stand up and shout: "This is my time and my place. I will accept the challenge."
~ *Marva Collins*

·····

Real education means to inspire people to live more abundantly, to learn to begin with life as they find it and make it better.
~ *Carter G. Woodson*

·····

Schoolhouses do not teach themselves -- piles of bricks and mortar and machinery do not send out children. [Education] is strengthened by long study and thought that breathes the real breath of life into boys and girls and makes them human.
~ *W.E. B. DuBois*

# EDUCATIONAL CATCH-PHRASES

# EDUCATION MAKES IT HAPPEN

*"In a world bursting with opportunity, the imagination is the wing of hope but education is your final destination."*
~*Unknown*

The following educational slogans can be used as a regular reference tool to continue to remind children about the importance of an education.

Each phrase is personalized with the understanding that *a good education* requires hard work, determination, and perseverance.

Used on a daily basis, these phrases provide the incentive to explain that with a good education any and everyone can become an asset to society instead of a liability.

**Education plus knowledge is the hallmark of each expression.**

## Slogans

- Education plus Knowledge: Encourages inquisitiveness for thinking, planning, and reasoning.

- Education plus Knowledge: Pumps up mental muscles, to bring out the natural genius in you.

- Education plus Knowledge: Opens windows of wonderment and growth to construct your own pyramid.

- Education plus Knowledge: Is your secret combination for professional employment and economic growth.

- Education plus Knowledge: Is the fabric for young minds to weave and develop their talents.

- Education plus Knowledge: Is a perfect backdrop for dreams and reality to meet.

- Education plus Knowledge: Are quality ingredients to melt into societal arena for career success -- a peck of unfaltering commitment, a pound of determination and a ton of hard work. When done, it's incredibly delightful when opportunity is served.

- Education plus Knowledge: Can stimulate an insatiable appetite to be the best you can be.

- Education plus Knowledge: Meticulously grooms you for today's technologically based world.

- Education plus Knowledge: Is a priceless gem to have in your treasure chest, one can travel further with it than without it.

- Education plus Knowledge: A steady diet provides many nectars to taste, doors to enter and explore, and infinite avenues to travel.

- Education plus Knowledge: Is your information highway where career consciousness evolves to envision dreams.

- Education plus Knowledge: Allows you to compete with many imaginations.

- Education plus Knowledge: Prepares one to pursue life's work intelligently.

- Education plus Knowledge: Your rock, your foundation, your insurance needed when opportunity and preparation meet.

- Education plus Knowledge: Yields a panorama of information to inspire the abstract expressionist within you.

- Education plus Knowledge: Allows everyone to make choices, the beauty of it is, it speaks to everyone.

- Education plus Knowledge: Nurtures and cultivates hidden talents.

- Education plus Knowledge: Prepares and propels when you persist and persevere.

- Education plus Knowledge: You can do more with it than without it.

- Education plus Knowledge: Can prevent you from wandering aimlessly through life.

- Education plus Knowledge: Yields an impressive resume, reflects beautifully with qualification.

- Education plus Knowledge: Reveals predictable and unpredictable potentials.

- Education plus Knowledge: Is a prestigious vehicle to carry you places you've never been. All you pay is attention.

## Closing Remarks

Once again, setting a positive tone in your classroom, in your home, or in any community location can be achieved by starting a child's day or program experience with a poem, expression or other words of encouragement. This not only stimulates the imagination but it also improved their ability to focus on learning and adds breadth and depth to the educational experience. A good education will make the difference in their success in life. If they believe they can achieve, they will achieve.

You may think getting an education is difficult. Try seeking employment without one.

■

Your commitment to achieve excellence
has to tie in with your actions and dedication.
The real passion is in the pen, voice and attitude.

*Sincerely,*

*Claritha D. Ingram*

# INDEX

A PATHWAY TO NOWHERE, 57
A POSITIVE APPROACH, 101
A POWERFUL TOOL, 59
A VOICE THAT SINGS, 32
AIM HIGH, 64
ALL ABOUT ME, 86
ARE YOU THINKING?, 29
ART OF IMAGINATION, 20
ART OF LISTENING, 21
ATTITUDE, 65

BOOK POWER, 75

CHANGE, 52
CONFESSION, 72
CONFIDENT, 43
CREATIVE THINKING, 36

DELIGHT YOURSELF, 47
DIRECT YOUR FUTURE, 71
DOOR OF OPPORTUNITY, 68
DREAMS, 51

EDUCATION IS, 46
EDUCATION MAKES IT HAPPEN, 124-127
EDUCATIONAL CATCH-PHRASES, 123
EVERYONE CAN'T BE, 41

FIND YOUR LIGHT, 67
FOOD FOR THOUGHT, 33
FROM A TEACHER TO STUDENTS, 28

GATEWAY TO SUCCESS, 56
GUIDANCE, 84
GUIDING STUDENTS, 19-36

HOLD FAST TO DREAMS, 74

I AM IN CHARGE, 63
I AM READY, 94
I AM THE GREATEST, 88
I GOT THIS, 98
IF, 73
INNER THOUGHTS, 93
INSPIRATION, 22
INSPIRATIONAL STEW, 23
INVISIBLE SHADOWS, 34
IT'S UP TO YOU, 40
IT'S YOUR FAULT, 50

LIFELONG LEARNER, 91
LITERARY GEMS, 102-122

MAKE IT HAPPEN, 89
MANAGE YOUR EDUCATION, 66
MOVING FORWARD, 96
MY PEOPLE, 74
MY PROFILE, 87

PASSIONATE, 92
POEMS FOR YOUNG SCHOLARS, 39-98
POSSIBILITY, 81
PRESS FORWARD, 49
PRICELESS GEM, 60
PROMOTE YOURSELF, 76

REFLECTIONS, 62
RULES AND PROCEDURES, 55

SCORING, 42
SELF-PROMOTION, 69
SIGNIFICANT, 97
SPECIAL, 78
SPOKEN WORDS, 26

TEACHING TIPS, 37-38
THE BEST YOU CAN BE, 77

THE BUILDER, 90
THE BUZZ, 45
THE CLASSROOM, 79
THINK, 53
THINK ABOUT IT, 25

WHAT IF, 85
WHAT IS KNOWLEDGE?, 48

WHAT'S BLOCKING THE
    LEARNING?, 83
WHY AM I HERE?, 82
WITTY WISDOM, 24
WORD POWER, 95

YOU ARE HISTORY IN THE
    MAKING, 61
YOU WANT POWER?, 70

# ABOUT THE AUTHOR

A retired classroom teacher, Claritha D. Ingram is a native of Memphis, Tennessee. She is a graduate of Carver High School and LeMoyne-Owen College in Memphis and Trevecca Nazarene University in Nashville. She served for more than 30 years as an elementary school teacher in the Memphis City School System followed by five years substitute teaching in a private/parochial middle school. A woman dedicated to getting the best from her students, she wrote poems and educational catch-phrases. She also clipped and used literary gems, thoughts to ponder and maxims from books and magazines to entice, train and motivate her students on a daily basis.

Her book, *Inspirational Stew: 150 Poems, Quotations and Maxims for Teachers, Parents and Caregivers to Encourage and Inspire Young People,* is her effort to share her winning strategy with others.

"All the loveliest things to say to students," Ingram believes, "come from simple, sweet, crisp, mind-altering expressions spoken with pizzazz and passion."

www.ingramcontent.com/pod-product-compliance
Lightning Source LLC
Chambersburg PA
CBHW071624170426
**43195CB00038B/2091**